STOREFRONT CHURCH

STOREFRONT CHURCH

John Patrick Shanley

THEATRE COMMUNICATIONS GROUP
NEW YORK
2014

The publication of *Storefront Church* by John Patrick Shanley, through TCG's Book Program, is made possible in part by the New York State Council on the Arts with the support of Governor Andrew Cuomo and the New York State Legislature.

TCG books are exclusively distributed to the book trade by Consortium Book Sales and Distribution.

LIBRARY OF CONGRESS CATALOGING-IN-PUBLICATION DATA
Shanley, John Patrick.
Storefront church / John Patrick Shanley.—First edition.
pages cm
ISBN 978-1-55936-441-6 (paperback)
ISBN 978-1-55936-759-2 (ebook)
1. Bronx (New York, N.Y.)—Economic conditions—Drama. 2. Clergy—Drama.
3. Spiritual life—Drama. I. Title.
PS3569.H3337S76   2014
812'.54—dc23   2014029523

Book design and composition by Lisa Govan
Cover design by John LaMacchia
Cover art by Dave McMacken

First Edition, September 2014

To Philip Seymour Hoffman,
that beautiful and private man,
who died too soon

Storefront Church received its world premiere at Atlantic Theater Company (Neil Pepe, Artistic Director; Jeffory Lawson, Managing Director) in New York City on June 11, 2012. It was directed by John Patrick Shanley; the set design was by Takeshi Kata, the costume design was by Alejo Vietti, the lighting design was by Matthew Richards, the sound design was by Bart Fasbender; the production stage manager was Alison DeSantis. The cast was:

ETHAN GOLDKLANG	Bob Dishy
REED VAN DRUYTEN	Zach Grenier
JESSIE CORTEZ	Tonya Pinkins
DONALDO CALDERON	Giancarlo Esposito
CHESTER KIMMICH	Ron Cephas Jones
TOM RAIDENBERG	Jordan Lage

Storefront Church opened at San Francisco Playhouse (Bill English, Artistic Director; Susi Damilano, Producing Director) on November 30, 2013. It was directed by Joy Carlin; the set design was by Bill English, the costume design was by Abra Berman, the lighting design was by David K.H. Elliott, the sound design was by Teddy Hulsker; the production stage manager was Tatjana Genser. The cast was:

ETHAN GOLDKLANG	Ray Reinhardt
REED VAN DRUYTEN	Rod Gnapp

If your church is sacred, our sister is, too. If our sister is not sacred, neither is your church.

—VICTOR HUGO,
The Hunchback of Notre-Dame

ETHAN: Let me ask you a question. What do you think makes somebody great?

REED: I have no idea.

ETHAN: Have you ever read *The Hunchback of Notre-Dame*?

REED: No. I'm not allowed to accept gifts.

ETHAN: What's the big deal? It's a cake. It's perishable. Do you read?

REED: Yes.

ETHAN: You oughta read *The Hunchback of Notre-Dame*. I'd lend it to you but I'm not done.

REED: That's all right.

ETHAN: Tells the story of this one nobody and you get everything. It's amazing how a story can make you feel the time. I mean, we're living in a time, right? This country was built by giants. They died and midgets moved in. Tiny people. We're walking around inside this republic like a nine-year-old boy wearing his father's suit. When the tiny people got in power, they changed what was taught in school. No great books, no big people. Everybody's tiny now. Well, let me tell you something. Greatness is real. And giants come along. You might be one. The opportunity is there, right now.

REED: I'm an officer of the bank. I can't be compromised by accepting gifts.

ETHAN: You're still on the cake? It's a cake. My wife made it for you. I can't eat it. With my arteries. You're stuck with it.

REED: Let's take a look at the numbers, shall we?

ETHAN: My best quarter's coming up.

REED: Obviously we go by what's here.

ETHAN: Right. We're the numbers people. But arithmetic is a limited language, my friend. Is it hot in here?

REED: I don't know.

ETHAN: You don't know if you're hot?!

REED: Any other documentation you want to include?

ETHAN: I'd just like to say, this picture's going to improve.

REED: You're the homeowner's spouse.

ETHAN: I'm her husband and her accountant.

REED: But the notes are in your wife's name.

ETHAN: I have a power of attorney. I can make a deal.

REED: What kind of offer can you make?

ETHAN: Here's the situation. Tax season's coming up. That's when I make my big money. I do taxes.

REED: Yes. I have your returns here . . .

ETHAN: See, I did those. I've been doing tax prep for forty years. I'll tell you my philosophy. My advice is my currency. When I give bad advice, it's a breach. People come to me 'cause I'm supposed to know. Bad advice is a debt.

REED: Ms. Cortez was fully informed of the terms before she signed these loans.

ETHAN: You know that? Were you there?

REED: The box is checked.

ETHAN: You don't know that.

REED: The box is checked.

ETHAN: Come on. Remember, you're talking to an accountant.

REED: Mr. Goldklang, let's call things by their right name. Accounting is a hobby for you.

ETHAN: What do you mean, a hobby?

REED: It's inconsequential. You're eligible for food stamps.

ETHAN: I don't get food stamps.

REED: You could. You're impoverished.

ETHAN: Fine. I'm poor. Help me.

REED: There are institutions for that.

ETHAN: This is an institution.

REED: Not that kind.

ETHAN: Do you have a family?

REED: I thought you were here to make an offer?

ETHAN: You don't have enough money? She needs an extension. I'll go into overdrive for tax season and catch her up. You can wait till April fifteenth for Chrissakes.

REED: Mmm. I'm not authorized to indefinitely postpone payment . . .

ETHAN: There's nothing indefinite about April fifteenth. She's been making payments for fourteen years. We're talking about four months.

REED: The account is already significantly in arrears.

ETHAN: So she's late. Haven't you ever been late for anything?

REED: I don't matter. It's the bank.

ETHAN: What do you mean, you don't matter? You're a human being. You matter.

Scene 2

The office of the Bronx borough president, Donaldo Calderon. The place has a cheap importance: wood paneling and wall sconces with frosted glass. There are awards, proclamations, a signed baseball bat, certificates from the chamber of commerce and so on. There's a Christmas tree in the process of being decorated.

    Donaldo is genial, good-looking, half-Italian, half-Puerto Rican, somewhere in his forties, a man very much in command of himself. He wears a suit. Maybe he could lose a few pounds. There's a cake box on his desk, and a slice of cake on a paper plate. He sits with Jessie Cortez. She's black, fifty-three, and dressed in Sunday clothes.

DONALDO: Mm, mm, mm! Jessie, thanks for the cake.
JESSIE: Donaldo, they're gonna throw me out of my house.
DONALDO: What?
JESSIE: Your mother said you would help me, Donaldo.
DONALDO: My mother is the Queen. If Mama said I will help you,
    I have no choice.
JESSIE: They're gonna throw me out of my house.
DONALDO: Who?

JESSIE: The bank.

DONALDO: You're behind?

JESSIE: Eight months.

DONALDO: Eight months? You shouldn't have let it go so long, Jessie.

JESSIE: They hit me with this maroon payment. Wiped me out.

DONALDO: What's that? Maroon payment? You mean balloon payment.

JESSIE: I call it a maroon payment 'cause my house is underwater so I'm marooned.

DONALDO: That's great except nobody knows what the hell you're talking about. What about Ethan? Can he help?

JESSIE: Ethan had a heart attack.

DONALDO: No. What do you mean?! When?

JESSIE: Tuesday. He got in a fight with the bank, then he couldn't breathe so they took him to Jacobi.

DONALDO: How is he?

JESSIE: He's got to take it easy now. He can't be going head-to-head with no bank.

DONALDO: What bank is it?

JESSIE: First Circle.

DONALDO: You serious? Circle Bank?

JESSIE: First Circle. That's right.

DONALDO: I'm meeting with the CEO of that Tuesday. They're financing a big project that's very good for us.

JESSIE: Who's us?

DONALDO: Everybody. The Bronx.

JESSIE: Well, I'm in the Bronx. Is it good for me?

DONALDO: Indirectly.

JESSIE: That means no.

DONALDO: Well, let's talk. Do you have a plan?

JESSIE: How you mean?

DONALDO: A payment plan.

JESSIE: They took this what you call balloon money, which was . . .

DONALDO (Overlapping): I don't call it that. That's what it's called.

JESSIE: It was all my savings. Now Ethan has heart disease. I'm up against the wall. You gotta help me.

DONALDO: So you have no . . . Do you have any assets?

JESSIE: The house.

DONALDO: Relatives?

JESSIE: Worse off than me.

DONALDO: You see what I'm driving at, Jessie. I can't walk into Circle Bank and just tell the CEO to forget about the money.

JESSIE: You don't need to talk to the CEO. Just my loan officer. Get him to ease up.

DONALDO: I'm not the right person for that.

JESSIE: You're my borough president.

DONALDO: And proud of it. But I have serious business with that bank and I will not jeopardize it by mucking around with some loan officer. It could be perceived as a conflict of interest.

JESSIE: How's that?

DONALDO: I have enemies, all right? The Latinos hate me 'cause my mother's Italian, and the Italians hate me because my father's Puerto Rican.

JESSIE: This isn't about you.

DONALDO: It is if I get into it.

JESSIE: Forget all that! You stop the bank! I have a sick man, no place to go, worked hard all my life. That house is all I've got to show.

DONALDO: I get it.

JESSIE: You get nothing. I lose that house, you're going to hell!

DONALDO: Me?

JESSIE: You took this job. You're my president. Some people say you got no compassion.

DONALDO: You know better than that.

JESSIE: I don't know anything since the politics got you.

DONALDO: What, you think politics turned my head?

JESSIE: I think it's cheapened your spirit.

DONALDO: I work hard for the Bronx!

JESSIE: Some people say you're packing your bags. Gonna jump ship for a pot of gold.

DONALDO: I have the right to build a career, Jessie.

JESSIE: Don't get huffy with me.

DONALDO: You didn't say this to my mother.

JESSIE: What point would there be? Your mother thinks you're a great man.

DONALDO: But you know better, huh?

JESSIE: YOU know better. You know what a great man is. You're
the other thing.

(Donaldo picks up the cake, starts eating.)

DONALDO: Tell you what. Why don't you talk to Councilman
Acosta. I'll give you the number.

JESSIE: Oh no you don't, Donaldo! You're gonna help me.

(He slams down the cake plate.)

DONALDO: Not while you're talking to me like that! Look,
I appreciate the cake, but my mandate is to get jobs into the
borough—that and land use.

JESSIE: My house is built on land.

DONALDO: If I help one person at the expense of many, I'm not
doing my job.

JESSIE: Come on. You'd be okay with helping one person if the
one person was you.

DONALDO: Look! The banks aren't interested in talking to me
about your debt.

JESSIE: You make them interested. This is economic war now!

DONALDO: Get out with that. It's not war just because you
messed up.

JESSIE: When they take your house, when they turn you out,
that's war.

DONALDO: Mamacita, please.

JESSIE: You're gonna have to pick a side, Donaldo.

DONALDO: You are not going to define me on your terms. I picked
my side long since, and it's with the everyday people. But
you have to understand that the Bronx needs the banks
more than the banks need the Bronx.

JESSIE: They want you to think that.

DONALDO: They got the money.

JESSIE: What's money? It won't save you when you're dying.

DONALDO: Maybe not, but you can't make a bank listen by going
on that there's an economic war. And I'll tell you something else. A man deserves to be paid. You borrow money
from a man, he deserves to be paid.

JESSIE: There's no man in this story. Show me a man. We're talking about a bank. Who's a bank?

DONALDO: Don't play dumb. It's people.

JESSIE: Not like me.

DONALDO: Just like you. A buncha people.

JESSIE: What kind of people? I wouldn't turn a woman out of her house if you put a gun to my head. Ain't a decent way to behave. Would you preach to a child to act that way? It takes a different class of human being to carry on like that. You know what? It takes a landlord to pull that shit.

DONALDO: Landlords have a right to make money.

JESSIE: And at Christmas time. *Feliz Navidad.* Who would choose to make money like that?

DONALDO: Just because it's not one face, one person giving you the money, you don't see it as a debt?

JESSIE: If a thing don't have a face, what is it?

DONALDO: A business!

JESSIE: If a bunch of people with no morality but money get together to jump on one person, I call that a gang.

DONALDO: It's time to look in the mirror and realize we have responsibilities, too.

JESSIE: You look in the mirror.

DONALDO: I take my measure every morning.

JESSIE: You're walking around in some big-shot fantasy.

DONALDO: I'm not walking around in anything but a pair of pants.

(Ethan staggers in. He's puffing. He has a beat-up old heavy schoolbag.)

ETHAN: Call off the dogs, you two! What's the ruckus?

JESSIE: Ethan!

ETHAN: Hey, Donaldo.

DONALDO: I thought you had a heart attack?

ETHAN: I did. So what? Life goes on. *(To Jessie)* I knew you'd come here. Leave off Donaldo.

JESSIE: I got this. You go home.

ETHAN: You got nothing. You go home.

JESSIE: He's gotta help us with the bank.

DONALDO: Talk to her, Ethan. I can't get involved in this one. It might give the appearance of impropriety.

ETHAN: No problem. I'm taking care of it.

JESSIE: You? You've got one foot in the kingdom come.

ETHAN: Jews don't have a kingdom come.

JESSIE: Another reason not to be a Jew.

ETHAN: Anti-Semite.

JESSIE: Then the more fool you for marrying me.

DONALDO: Ethan, your doctor know you're out?

ETHAN: Stedman don't care where I am as long as I get the bill. How's the cake?

JESSIE: You can't have any.

(Ethan gets a fork.)

ETHAN: No? Watch me. *(Sings a few bars of "If I Were a Rich Man," dancing over to the cake)*

JESSIE: Stay away from that cake. Ethan! Don't eat that cake! There's five eggs in there, and two sticks of butter! Don't eat that cake, I said! He's eating the cake.

DONALDO: I can see that.

(Ethan eats.)

ETHAN: Anyway, she's not gonna lose the house.

JESSIE: How do you know?

ETHAN *(Referring to the cake)*: This is too good.

JESSIE: Same cake I make every day.

ETHAN: I take each cake as it comes.

JESSIE: Why am I not gonna lose my house?

ETHAN: Life insurance.

DONALDO: You have life insurance?

ETHAN: I do.

DONALDO: There you go. The cash-convertible kind?

ETHAN: No, the drop-dead kind. I'm worth two hundred and fifty grand dead and the mortgage is only one-eighty. Do the math. So let me eat cake, you see what I'm saying?

DONALDO: You should be home.

ETHAN: I stay home and take the meds, I could live long enough to be evicted.

JESSIE: Goddamn landlords.

ETHAN: What are you talking about landlords? You ARE a land-lord.

DONALDO: What? Who's a landlord?

ETHAN: Her. Jessie.

DONALDO: She is?

JESSIE: Bullshit!

ETHAN: You have a tenant. That makes you a landlord.

DONALDO: You have a tenant? That changes the picture. So you have income there.

JESSIE: There's no income. He can't pay.

ETHAN: Goes way beyond not paying. *(To Jessie)* You didn't tell him, did you? Jessie loaned the tenant money. She took out a second mortgage, thirty thousand dollars, and gave it to this guy to renovate.

DONALDO: Renovate what?

ETHAN: The old laundry downstairs.

DONALDO: He's opening up a laundromat?

JESSIE *(Overlapping)*: No laundromat, it's a church. He's made it over into a storefront church.

(Donaldo registers that.)

DONALDO: A church?

JESSIE: Yeah.

DONALDO: He's a reverend?

JESSIE: Pentecostal.

ETHAN: The quietest Pentecostal I've ever seen.

JESSIE: He's been down.

ETHAN: He has no congregation. *(To Donaldo)* The second mort-gage is just hanging there, but this reverend . . .

DONALDO: What's his name?

JESSIE: Chester Kimmich.

DONALDO: I don't know him.

ETHAN: He's a good ten months behind.

DONALDO: Have you pressed him?

ETHAN: She won't do it.

JESSIE: I can't do that.

DONALDO: Why not?

JESSIE: He's . . . He's not an ordinary man.

DONALDO: Is that right? In what way is he special?

JESSIE: He carries the weight of many.

ETHAN: She brings him food. She's feeding the guy.

JESSIE: Donaldo, there is another world and you know it. Your father knew it, too.

DONALDO: My father never saw his calling as a reason not to pay his rent.

JESSIE: This man is bound up with something beyond the everyday. He has a greatness.

DONALDO: Oh, I'm not great but this deadbeat's got the goods, huh?

JESSIE: He's taking care of what you're not.

DONALDO: You have to talk to this guy, Jessie. What's his name?

ETHAN: Chester Kimmich.

DONALDO: You have to talk to this Chester Kimmich.

JESSIE: About what?

DONALDO: On the subject of responsibility. He's put you in a position.

ETHAN: He spent every dime she gave him fixing the place up into a church, then never held a service.

JESSIE: The reverend doesn't have to do with the matter at hand. It's the bank that's on me.

DONALDO: The first question a loan officer is going to ask is why you haven't collected the rent from your tenant. And I'll tell you what he's going to think. He's going to think you're taking the money in cash and stiffing the bank.

JESSIE: Only a thief would think like that!

ETHAN: A lotta people think like that. I think like that.

JESSIE: You think I'm pocketing money?

DONALDO: No, but he might be. A storefront church is a cash business.

JESSIE: It's not a business. It's a church.

ETHAN: Barely.

DONALDO: Talk to him.

JESSIE: I can't do it. I get done in with shame.

DONALDO: What do you got to be ashamed of? He's the one at fault.

JESSIE: Everybody's got something to be ashamed of.

ETHAN: Jews call it "the air we breathe."

DONALDO: Is he guilt-trippin' you somehow?

JESSIE: No. There's a weight on him he carries for me that makes me ashamed.

DONALDO: I don't know what to say to that. That just sounds crazy.

ETHAN: She won't let me talk to him.

JESSIE: It's not a simple thing.

DONALDO: I think you're building this up beyond what it is. You should never have extended yourself financially, Jessie. You were foolish and it's come back to bite you. You had no business borrowing money for a romantic purpose.

JESSIE: Romantic?

ETHAN: Wait a minute. Is that why you're feeding that bastid? Romance?

JESSIE *(To Ethan)*: Are you serious?! Get real!

ETHAN: I'll kill you both!

DONALDO: Don't get excited. I'm talking about religion. I've seen people get a crush on religion many's the time, and do things that made no sense in the light of day.

JESSIE: What makes sense to me in this world used to make sense to you.

DONALDO: When I was a kid.

JESSIE: You had a sense of sin when you were a child.

DONALDO: I still do, but admit it. You got carried away.

JESSIE: You used to get carried away, too.

DONALDO: And my father before me. But I paid a price one too many times, Jessie. I can't afford to get high on righteousness anymore. I gave that up the day I found my manhood. It's a vice to love righteousness too much.

JESSIE: How can righteousness be a vice?

DONALDO: When other people have to pay for it, it's a vice.

JESSIE: Some people call that pitching in. Doing your part.

DONALDO: For what? A great man? We all want to believe somebody's got the torch. Some people take advantage. This Chester Kimmich, he's out of line. He needs to be served.

JESSIE: Talk to him then. I don't mind. Take him in. His true intention runs through him like a fire. It's you I can't see to the bottom of no more, Donaldo. You've become a bottle

of smoke from all the rooms you've been in. Your father's
been dead too long and maybe you've lost your way.

DONALDO: You're the one's taken money and don't have it to give
back. You're the one that's come to ME for help. It's easy to
stay in the shallow waters and judge those that go into the
deep for you. I've been in many rooms it's true, but I went
into those rooms for everyday folks in trouble, and I dealt
with the dirt and confusion I found there.

ETHAN: Politics.

DONALDO: That's right. Politics. You look down on it till you
need it. Jessie, it's called growing up.

JESSIE: Don't tell the woman who combed the nits out of your
hair to grow up! Now my husband is short of breath . . .

ETHAN (Overlapping): Nobody needs to do anything anyway . . .

JESSIE: Shut up! My husband is short of breath and can't go on
like Clarence Thomas with these people . . .

ETHAN (Overlapping): You don't mean Clarence Thomas. He
never says anything. You mean Clarence Darrow.

JESSIE: I mean be quiet!

ETHAN: This cake is gonna kill me and solve the problem.

JESSIE: Would you shut up?!

DONALDO: Jesus Christ, get a grip!

JESSIE: Talk to the loan officer!

DONALDO: It's a conflict of interest.

JESSIE: Your mother co-signed the loan.

DONALDO: What? What? My mother what?

JESSIE: Your mother co-signed the loan. She put up the condo
you gave her. She liked the idea of a church. Reminded her
of your dad. (Pause)

DONALDO: Goddammit! She did not!! (Pause) She did?

JESSIE: She did.

DONALDO: All right. Goddammit. Well, I'm not talking to any
loan officer till I talk to this fraud preacher!

ETHAN (Overlapping): About the loan officer. You might want to
know . . .

DONALDO: What?

ETHAN: The loan officer. His wife shot him in the face.

DONALDO: Who?

JESSIE: Back up. What did you say?

ETHAN: The loan officer.

DONALDO: Who shot who in the face?

ETHAN: His wife. It was in the *Post* a couple of years ago. They were going through a divorce and she shot him in the face. About money. You can see it. He's blind in one eye, and the side of his face is a little dead.

JESSIE: A man with half his face dead who throws women in the gutter at Christmas. That's a movie. That's what we're dealing with, Donaldo.

DONALDO: I'm making a mistake getting into this. All right. I'll do my best and leave the rest. I'll talk to the reverend. I'll talk to the bank.

JESSIE: Praise God!

ETHAN: And pass the ammunition.

(Blackout.)

Scene 3

A park bench. Reed enters in a winter coat, carrying a valise and a cup of coffee. Music. Something like Nick Cave singing "Into My Arms." Reed sits on a bench, takes out Ethan's copy of The Hunchback of Notre-Dame, *reads. He starts to cry silently. It snows a few flakes. It snows heavier. He puts the book away and just sits there. He touches his face a couple of times. He gets up and starts to go. He looks back at the empty bench. The lights fade.*

Scene 4

A small storefront church. It's dark, lit only by a small dirty window that faces an alley. There are eleven chairs and a cheap electric piano. A couple of lamps sit on card tables. A beat-up, steel-cut door to the right opens onto the street. A curtain, to the left, leads to other rooms.

    Sitting backward in one of the chairs is Chester Kimmich. He's somewhere in his middle years, whatever they are. I don't know how old he is. I don't care how old he is. He's a man who's seen more than he wanted to. The light from the lone window falls on him. He rests his head against his hands on the chair's back. A knock. Chester doesn't respond. The door opens, permitting light from the street.

    Donaldo enters in a coat and scarf, carrying two coffees.

DONALDO: Hello? All right if I come in? *(Joking weakly)* Don't have a gun, do you? Do you mind a visitor? I'm a friend of your landlady, Jessie Cortez. My name's Donaldo Calderon. I'm the borough president. Mind if I take off my coat? I'm all bundled up against the weather. Dark in here. *(Turns on a lamp)* That's a bit better. I'm assuming you're the reverend, Chester Kimmich. Do I have that right?

CHESTER: Yes, sir.

DONALDO: Good. Glad to talk with you.

CHESTER: Would you mind? I don't feel like talking.

DONALDO: Brought you a coffee.

CHESTER: Don't want coffee.

DONALDO: Suit yourself. My father was a pastor, had a little congregation over on West Farms. The elevated train would try to drown him out but he would drown out the elevated train. He was a great man. For a time, I thought I'd set up like him, but I never did. Went into political work instead. And here I am, you know, making my way up the ladder. You've put Miss Cortez in a bind, Reverend Kimmich. She's in a bind. (Pause) Is there something wrong?

CHESTER: You'd better just tell me.

DONALDO: Tell you what?

CHESTER: What you want.

DONALDO: Well, I'm here for Jessie Cortez because you owe her money and she owes the bank money.

CHESTER: I don't have any money.

DONALDO: Well, what are you doing, Chester? I mean are you planning to just do nothing till the world comes and gets you?

CHESTER: I don't know.

DONALDO: 'Cause the world is coming. If you sit down and don't get up, eventually that's what takes place. So it's better to take action, you know?

CHESTER: What kind of action?

DONALDO: You could leave. Then Jessie could rent this place out to somebody who settles up once a month. Do you like that idea?

CHESTER: Why are you here?

DONALDO: I told you.

CHESTER: You'd better head home.

DONALDO: Your landlady asked me to come.

CHESTER: You always do what folks ask?

DONALDO: No. But in this case, you being a reverend, I thought it might be good to take you in. Take your measure.

CHESTER: I can't help you.

DONALDO: It's not me that needs help.

CHESTER: Nobody says that who knows anything.

DONALDO: Look. Jessie's an old friend. She went to my mother, and my mother wants me to help her. That's why I'm here. This isn't what I usually do. I'm borough president.

CHESTER: What's that?

DONALDO: It's a political job. I was elected. I'm supposed to bring business to the Bronx. Are you conducting services here?

CHESTER: Not yet.

DONALDO: What's holding you up?

CHESTER: I ran into a problem.

DONALDO: Well, you're talking to the right man because I solve problems. What's in the way?

CHESTER: Me. I guess. Or worse.

DONALDO: Or worse? Would that be the devil? And don't think I'm drawing you out to make a fool of you. I believe in the devil. I saw him in a dream when I was a boy. He had a carriage and his horses ran backwards. I know the devil to be real.

CHESTER: I don't know.

DONALDO: Well, what do you know, Chester?

CHESTER: Devil always looks like somebody else.

DONALDO: I admit I'm getting a little frustrated here. If I talk to the bank after this, I don't know what to say. You're not being forthcoming. You have put an honest woman in jeopardy. You took her money and I have to say, if this is the renovation you did, it don't look like much. Capital improvements usually show. This place looks ragged.

CHESTER: Ran out of money. Couldn't finish.

DONALDO: So what are you at?

CHESTER: What do you mean?

DONALDO: What's the plan?

CHESTER: I'm struggling with the thing in front of me.

DONALDO: And what would that be?

CHESTER: Well. There's a big black hole in the floor in front of me and so I can't make my way.

DONALDO: A big black hole?

CHESTER: That's right.

DONALDO: You're depressed.

CHESTER: You say your father was a pastor?

DONALDO: That's right.

CHESTER: I'm not talking about depression. I'm talking about a hole in the road before me, big, deep and getting bigger, and it's a test and a trial and I am bound up here with no way forward. Do you understand me as your father would understand me?

DONALDO: Yeah.

CHESTER: Just as you have been sent to me this day. In the same way as that.

DONALDO: Maybe I'm your wake-up call.

CHESTER: I'd welcome it. There's a hole in the ground in front of me, Donaldo. What should I do? Tell me and I'll do it. I'm standing ready. I can't hold a service because of the hole. I can't breathe in the light of day without pain because of the hole. I can't have a woman or taste my bread or even weep . . . because of this hole that opened up on my path. What should I do?

DONALDO: I can't answer that.

CHESTER: Why not?

DONALDO: That kind of thing has got to come from you.

CHESTER: Then it's like I thought. You're not my wake-up call. I am awake. I am your wake-up call. You ready for it? Here it comes. Wake up. Now put on your coat and go home.

DONALDO: It's been my experience that men and women bring different things to the table. My mother was a practical woman. My father was not a practical man. My father told me about heaven and the devil and he could recite poetry like silver and gold and I looked up to him like you would look up at a mountain. I admired him so. He was a good man, and when he died, even in his casket he spread peace and love to the room around him. As a loving son, I wanted to be just like my daddy. I memorized poetry and thought about good and bad, read the Bible, took classes . . . And one day, I saw my momma was crying, and I asked her why. She said she was exhausted. She had two jobs, raised six kids, had some diabetes. And I realized she had carried my father all his life, and now she was carrying me. Poor woman was half dead. That's when I gave up the idea of the ministry and decided to help people in THIS world.

CHESTER: Do you?

DONALDO: Sometimes. I'm trying to now. This woman upstairs is carrying you, Chester. And it's breaking her.

CHESTER: Did your mother doubt your father's calling?

DONALDO: She's never said. But maybe I did.

CHESTER: It's a fair question, who's carrying who in this world.

DONALDO: But at least my father did his work, and took up the collection. You're just sitting here.

CHESTER: Yes.

DONALDO: You're just sitting with it.

CHESTER: That's right. I'm sitting with it.

DONALDO: Well, I couldn't do that and look in the mirror.

CHESTER: Should anybody do it? Should anybody sit with it? What are you doing? What's a borough president?

DONALDO: I drum up business for the borough. It's a job. If I do well with it, it's a step. And I have done well with it.

CHESTER: So you're stepping.

DONALDO: Mr. Kimmich, are you going to get off your ass anytime soon?

CHESTER: Don't know.

DONALDO: What took thirty thousand dollars? This place looks like hell.

CHESTER: The floor was rotted. Money don't go far.

DONALDO: And you have nothing put aside?

CHESTER: As I told you, no.

DONALDO: I'll just put it to you then. Get out of here or do your work.

CHESTER: I'm doing my work. I'll make a deal with you. If you leave me alone, I'll leave you alone.

DONALDO: Me? You're not in my way. You're not bothering me.

CHESTER: Is that right? You look bothered.

DONALDO: You got it wrong. Am I bothering you?

CHESTER: You're slowing me down.

DONALDO: From sitting with it.

CHESTER: That's right.

DONALDO: Oh, this is outrageous, Chester! You're screwing an innocent woman out of her house and home in the name of nobility, and there ain't a noble thing about it! You need to face up. She believes in you! She believes you are engaged in a higher purpose. Jessie Cortez works in a hospital. Has all her life. Breaks her ass taking care of sick people. What do you do? Why do you deserve to suck her dry? It's unjust! Does the idea of justice hold any weight with you?

CHESTER: I don't know about justice.

DONALDO: Why not?

CHESTER: It's beyond me.

DONALDO: Her husband had a heart attack. He's hoping he'll die so she gets insurance money. That's what's going on upstairs while you're downstairs sitting on your hands.

CHESTER: You said if I sat here long enough, the world would come to me. Well, you're the first one in the door. What's the world got to say?

DONALDO: That you should be ashamed! You're the kind that holds all the good ones back. High-minded thief stealing from kindness.

CHESTER: Are you one of the good ones?

DONALDO: Damn right! Some of us are trying to make something of ourselves!

CHESTER: Not like your dad.

DONALDO: What did you say?!

CHESTER: You heard me.

DONALDO: Don't even mention my father in the same room as yourself! My father put out his hands to a world of people!

CHESTER: And yet you doubted him when he put his hand out to you.

DONALDO: So what?! What son hasn't doubted his father? May he rest in peace and kindness.

CHESTER: Maybe he will if you let him. It's funny though.

DONALDO: What?

CHESTER: You say one day you noticed your mother was carrying all the weight and your father had a free pass.

DONALDO: To some degree.

CHESTER: Strange something killed your dad and momma's still with us. For all her troubles.

DONALDO: He had a stroke.

CHESTER: Like I said. Justice is beyond me. Beyond the human mind.

DONALDO: It all depends how you tell the story.

CHESTER: You told it your way, got the lesson you wanted. Walked away from the life of the spirit. Took up politics.

DONALDO: That's right. I'm a politician. And that means I don't say everything I feel. But just because I don't say out loud the wellsprings of my conviction doesn't lessen their power.

CHESTER: So you have conviction.

DONALDO: Absolutely.

CHESTER: I envy you that.

DONALDO: Don't you?

CHESTER: I don't know. Passion feels good though.

DONALDO: If I have a fire in my belly today, you put it there.

CHESTER: And how did I do that?

DONALDO: By your actions.

CHESTER: You mean sitting here?

DONALDO: It's just the two of us, so I say it right out. I have a disgust and rage at the exploitation of ignorant people by religion.

CHESTER: Okay.

DONALDO: Seen it all my life. People afraid of death, can't face it, so they listen to your lies and platitudes while you pick their pockets.

CHESTER: But I'm not even taking up a collection.

DONALDO: There's more than one way to victimize people! You're profiting off a naive woman's trust.

CHESTER: Isn't that what the bank did?

DONALDO: The bank acted in good faith!

CHESTER: So you're on the bank's side.

DONALDO: I'm here for the woman upstairs!

CHESTER: But you agree with the bank. You have kids?

DONALDO: Two boys.

CHESTER: They look up to you?

DONALDO: Of course.

CHESTER: You ever worry what they're looking up at?

DONALDO: No.

CHESTER: Maybe you should worry more.

DONALDO: Like you? You were sitting in the dark when I walked in.

CHESTER: There's honor in the dark.

DONALDO: Look, I promised Jessie I'd do my best with you . . .

CHESTER: You do your best with me, the bank will suffer.

DONALDO: I won't allow that to happen.

CHESTER: So you're protecting the bank, not the woman.

DONALDO: No.

CHESTER: I'm from New Orleans. Hadda church. Then Katrina hit. When I went back, my life was gone. Hurricane.

DONALDO: Sorry to hear that.

CHESTER: I had a story, but that story was built on a levee and the levee gave out. I came up north, but then this hole opened up. I had to stop. I was afraid but I had to stop anyway.

DONALDO: But maybe that's just an evil voice, Chester. A voice to be pushed aside. You heard the call to open a church and does it make sense God would contradict Himself, change His mind? It doesn't make any sense. God doesn't change His mind.

CHESTER: The experience of life is ongoing. Contradictions arise, uncomfortable as that may be.

DONALDO: God walks in a straight line.

CHESTER: God rages all over the sky! I'm here to tell you that much.

DONALDO: The Bronx doesn't need another church. It needs money.

CHESTER: Just go.

DONALDO: You go! You're the fraud.

CHESTER: No doubt you're right.

DONALDO: And don't agree with me. Don't pose as civil! You're a squatter. Will you leave this place and let Jessie get on with a new tenant?

CHESTER: No.

DONALDO: Then come Sunday hold a service! Pass the plate. It's Christmas. People are generous at this season. Especially poor people.

CHESTER: Cynical remark.

DONALDO: You bring it out in me.

CHESTER: I couldn't look them in the eye and pass the plate.

DONALDO: Why not?

CHESTER: Because my Lord in heaven tells me wait.

DONALDO: Wait for what? It doesn't make any sense.

CHESTER: Nobody wants to sit with it. I don't know what to do and as long as that is the case, I will stand still!

DONALDO: If I lived my life like that, I wouldn't get anything done.

CHESTER: Do you get anything done?

DONALDO: Of course. Do you talk to anybody?

CHESTER: No.

DONALDO: Jessie?

CHESTER: She brings me supper. I thank her.

DONALDO: That woman makes a chocolate cake every day of her life so children will come by. She talks to them about every little thing.

CHESTER: And you're her champion.

DONALDO: I was one of those children.

CHESTER: And look at you now. I see the jackal in your eye, Donaldo. Politics. You think politics will protect you?

DONALDO: Politics is an adult activity. Look. Do you think when you said a hole opened in the ground in front of you, do you think I don't know about that?

CHESTER: And what do you do?

DONALDO: I take action.

CHESTER: How you know what action to take?

DONALDO: I don't, but doing something is better than doing nothing. I'm here to tell you. Doing something works.

CHESTER: You're like a blind man with a chainsaw.

DONALDO: And you're just paralyzed!

CHESTER: This world is on fire, buying and selling. People yelling, "Action must be taken." Why? A voice came to me and said, "Chester, make a church for me, a little storefront church, a station of sincerity." I set about it. I'm here. The chairs are set up. I have a piano there. But then the voice came again. And the voice said, "Look down, Chester." And I did. And there was a broken place between me and the future. I'm not going to ignore that.

DONALDO: Well, you think a lot of yourself that God speaks to you. What if nobody gives a damn what you do and it don't matter that you were born?

CHESTER: You're in more trouble than me.

DONALDO: Nobody cares whether this twelve-chair church opens or not.

CHESTER: You seem to.

DONALDO: I got dragged into this.

CHESTER: By your mother.

DONALDO: She's a sucker for religion. I'm not.

CHESTER: I think you're yelling in the mirror.

DONALDO: I might as well be.

CHESTER: I see a man yelling at his father.

DONALDO: You see nothing!

CHESTER: And maybe you've wasted every day of your life since you stepped away from him.

DONALDO: I caught my mother before she hit the ground. That's what I chose to do and I'd do it again. Shit, I am doing it again. She co-signed the loan on this place.

CHESTER: Did she?

DONALDO: Yes. Damn fool.

CHESTER: What did your father want for you? What do you want for your sons?

DONALDO: He wanted me to lead an upright life. I lead an upright life!

CHESTER: Why?

DONALDO: Because I have a conscience.

CHESTER: If you let conscience get the upper hand, you're done.

DONALDO: Are you done?

CHESTER: I don't know. There's a moral force. It supersedes self-interest and personally terrifies me. But that's the ministry I seek.

DONALDO: I'm not ashamed of what I do.

CHESTER: Lack of shame is not the same as innocence. Ask any prostitute.

DONALDO: WHAT DID YOU SAY?! You wanna get your face smacked?

CHESTER: Easy now.

DONALDO: You can't just say whatever comes into your head.

CHESTER: Well, look at that. The politician has left the building.

DONALDO: Just 'cause I have social skills don't think you can walk on me.

CHESTER: Wait!

DONALDO: What is it?

CHESTER: Something just moved. You're affecting me. I'm affected. Would you come to my service?

DONALDO: What?

CHESTER: If I had a service, would you come?

DONALDO: How did we get to that? I have a church I attend.

CHESTER: So you wouldn't?

DONALDO: I didn't say that.

CHESTER: Will you come if I have a service?

DONALDO: I'll tell you what. All right, you have a service, I'll come.

CHESTER: Good.

DONALDO: But you'd better have the Word, you understand me? You'd better have the news from the Man himself.

CHESTER: All right.

DONALDO: Now if you'll excuse me, I guess, since I've made no headway here, I'm going to go talk to Jessie's banker. Maybe he's reasonable.

CHESTER: Maybe. Why not ask him to the service, too?

DONALDO: Bring the loan officer here?

CHESTER: Yes.

DONALDO: What for? A banker is money first. Banker comes, he'll be interested in the collection.

CHESTER: Let him look. Next Sunday, ten o'clock. That be all right? Can you do that?

DONALDO: I can do it. But I can't speak for anybody else.

CHESTER: Your best will be good enough.

DONALDO: All right. Can I ask you?

CHESTER: What?

DONALDO: You've been sitting here for what, ten months. Why all of a sudden are you willing to have a service?

CHESTER: I always was willing. Only now I see a step forward. One step.

DONALDO: I don't.

CHESTER: Maybe that hole's moving over your way.

(Donaldo goes to the door.)

DONALDO: Ten o'clock this Sunday?

CHESTER: That's right.

DONALDO: Hope you know what you're doing.

CHESTER: I don't. That's faith.

(Donaldo goes.)

ACT TWO

Scene 1

A bank CEO, Mr. Tom Raidenberg, sits in his office. A nice desk and chairs. On the desk is a gift basket holding a foot-high gingerbread house. Donaldo has just walked in.

TOM: Sit, please sit.

DONALDO: Thanks.

TOM: What was that email yesterday?

DONALDO: Just a thought.

TOM: Seemed a little cool.

DONALDO: Not at all. What do we have here?

TOM: A gingerbread house.

DONALDO: Takes me back. That's a cute one.

TOM: It's a gift for my son.

DONALDO: Oh, he'll like that. My boys would, too.

TOM: Yes.

DONALDO: Can I ask where you got it?

TOM: Full disclosure, my secretary gave it to me to give to him. I wouldn't give the boy sweets. Not this much anyway. My wife would kill me. She's a health nut. Asian.

DONALDO: Kids love sugar.

TOM: Yes, they do. Hell, I love sugar. You know, I can't bring this home. Take a piece.

DONALDO: No, thanks.

TOM: You'd be doing my son a favor.

DONALDO: Not right now.

TOM: Well then, I guess it falls to me. *(He breaks off a piece)* So how's our little project looking, Mr. Calderon?

DONALDO: Please. Donaldo.

TOM: Of course, Donaldo. How's it looking?

DONALDO: What can I say? The proposal is making its way through the system.

TOM: The mayor's behind this one hundred percent.

DONALDO: I know, Tom. That's actually been a bit of a stumbling block. The city council doesn't utterly love the mayor right now. He's pushed them around a bit.

TOM: But there is general agreement this would be great for the Bronx?

DONALDO: There's some agreement. I wouldn't call it general.

TOM: Three hundred million dollars comes into the borough, a huge facility that's been sitting empty for a decade comes to life, businesses come in, jobs are created. What's the downside?

DONALDO: Quality of life.

TOM: You're desperate for jobs.

DONALDO: But these are minimum wage jobs. My constituents are sick of that.

TOM: They'd rather be unemployed?

DONALDO: Would that be enough for your son? A minimum wage job?

TOM: Maybe, starting out.

DONALDO: What if he weren't starting out? What if you had to wake up and know this is it. "This is my life. I'm a grown man working for minimum wage."

(Tom rips off another piece of the house.)

TOM: Is this your point of view?

DONALDO: No, but I'm not just me, if you know what I mean. I have to be a representative voice. I'm gathering information, reactions from my people. Opinions are still coming in.

TOM: Well, what's the alternative? What would they do with the building? Let it rot?

DONALDO: Some groups would rather see it made into a community center than a mall.

TOM: That would be a pretty big community center.

DONALDO: Yes, it would. Biggest in the city.

TOM: I mean, what does that say? Here you have a population, highest unemployment rate in the city, and when given the choice between jobs and, I don't know what, basketball, they choose basketball?

DONALDO: It says community is important to these people, maybe more important than a minimum wage job in a chain store.

(Tom rips off another piece of the house.)

TOM: You're close with the mayor, aren't you?

DONALDO: He's been good to me.

TOM: Do you want this deal to go through?

DONALDO: I'm supposed to bring business into the borough. This would be a coup. But this project needs to feel like the Bronx, not just Anywhere, USA. And malls don't age that well.

TOM: This isn't your average mall. The building itself has so much character.

DONALDO: You're right. It's an old building. It has beauty. But should its character be seen as a commercial opportunity or a civic responsibility? Are we putting a fine face on something with no soul? That's the question I'm being hit with.

TOM: You mentioned basketball . . .

DONALDO: What are you talking about? You mentioned basketball.

TOM: But what about that? What if a certain percentage of the space were earmarked for community-style activities like basketball?

DONALDO: That would help. How much?

TOM: Ten percent?

DONALDO: Fifteen.

TOM: Fifteen.

DONALDO: Is basketball code?

TOM: No, basketball is not code.

DONALDO: Okay, I'll bring this to the council. It might convince some people.

(Tom rips off another piece of the house, offers it to Donaldo.)

TOM: Does it convince you?

DONALDO: I don't have a vote.

TOM: They'll listen to you. It's your borough. *(Referring to the gingerbread)* Take a piece. I don't want to be the only bad guy here. Take it.

(Donaldo takes it and eats.)

DONALDO: Thanks.

TOM: Earmarking fifteen percent for community, does it convince you?

DONALDO: Me? Don't worry about me. I'm sold.

TOM: Don't bullshit me. I'm a salesman. Something's different. Our last meeting, you were totally enthusiastic. Now I'm seeing this reluctance. What's that about?

DONALDO: I'm sorry. You threw me. I came here to meet with a loan officer about something else. I wasn't prepared to sit down with you.

TOM: That's all?

DONALDO: That's it.

TOM: Well, damn. I'm sorry I ambushed you. It was impulsive. I heard you were here. I'm excited about the deal.

DONALDO: No problem, but that's why I may seem unsettled. Actually, I'm going to be late for my appointment.

TOM: Don't worry about the loan officer. He's on his way.

DONALDO: Here? What do you mean?

TOM: He's coming up. Reed Van Druyten.

DONALDO: Do you think that's wise?

TOM: It's fine. Do you know this guy?

DONALDO: No.

TOM: I've laid eyes on him, that's about it, but he's got a real history. He was CFO of a major appliance company, got bought out, made a killing, and then thought he was a high roller. Got a supermodel girlfriend, the whole thing. Only he was married, and when he filed for divorce, his wife— ding-dong, bang—shot him in the face. *(Tears off another piece of the house)* Have another piece.

DONALDO: Thanks.

TOM: Big trial. He was in a coma, woke up, his wife's in prison, the model's gone—Russian—the economy crashed, his portfolio's in ruins. So now he's a working stiff again, loan officer for First Circle. Some story, huh?

DONALDO: Yeah.

(Intercom buzzer. Tom answers.)

TOM: Yes?

WOMAN'S VOICE: Mr. Van Druyten.

TOM: Wait a beat and send him in. *(To Donaldo)* Try not to stare at his face. There's a little palsy there.

DONALDO: I was meeting him on a personal matter, Tom. I don't want an appearance of impropriety.

TOM: Come on. You're not looking to enrich yourself. I looked into it. You're here for one of your constituents. Let's see if we can make some rain.

(Reed enters with an accordion folder.)

Reed Van Druyten.

REED: Hello, Mr. Raidenberg.

TOM: This is Donaldo Calderon, Bronx borough president. Donaldo, this is Reed Van Druyten.

DONALDO: Nice to meet you, Reed.

TOM *(To Donaldo)*: Sit, sit. *(Hands Reed a piece of gingerbread)* Reed, eat this. It's gingerbread. How's it going?

REED: Fine.

TOM: Thanks for coming up. I don't get down to the floor enough, I know that. How's the refi effort going?

REED: Most people don't meet the requirements.

TOM *(To Donaldo)*: We're reaching out to the community, trying to keep some of these borrowers in their homes, but it's challenging.

REED: Aaaaa. There's an income and net worth window. The guidelines are pretty specific. Too much, we can't do it. Too little, same thing. Frankly, we're choking on the volume of foreclosures. Ms. Cortez has authorized me to speak to you about her debt.

TOM: How's it look?

REED: Aaaa. Not too promising. There are two mortgages . . . The borrower's income meets the low threshold. That's good. But the bottom line is the place went underwater in the crash, and no matter how we modify the mortgages, I don't think Ms. Cortez can handle it. It was the second mortgage that really took her down. Thirty thousand dollars for capital improvements on a mixed-use building, but it didn't result in any income. Aaaa, there IS a guarantor on the second mortgage and we could . . .

TOM *(Interrupting)*: Thanks, Reed. I wonder what the capital improvements were for? Do you know, Donaldo?

DONALDO: It's a church.

TOM: What?

DONALDO: It's a little storefront church.

TOM: What exactly is a storefront church?

DONALDO: In these poor neighborhoods it's not uncommon for somebody to set up a little ministry in a storefront. A dozen chairs, a little piano, put on a service, pass the hat.

TOM: Does that make money?

DONALDO: Some do better than others. None of them make much.

TOM: How's this one do?

DONALDO: This one never opened at all.

TOM: Can we write this off as a small business loan?

REED: That's not how she applied for it.

TOM: It sounds like that's what it really is.

DONALDO: She handed him the money for a renovation.

TOM: Who?

DONALDO: A preacher.

TOM: Was the work done?

DONALDO: Yes.

TOM: Maybe we can reverse-engineer this into a small business loan that went south and write it off.

DONALDO: Would that be aboveboard?

TOM: I don't know. We won't do it otherwise. Write it up that way, Reed, run it by legal. Come up with a checklist of what we'll need from the client. Nancy can help you with this. Nancy can do anything. She's the pretty black woman you passed on the way in. Shoot me an email and tell me how it looks.

REED: We do have a guarantor on the loan.

(Tom interrupts forcefully, even brutally.)

TOM: Don't bother with the guarantor. It's not germane.

(Reed gets up to go.)

REED: All right. I met with Ms. Cortez' husband. Do you know him?

DONALDO: Yes.

(Reed pulls out the thick paperback.)

REED: He got sick in my office and left this.

(Donaldo takes the book.)

DONALDO: *The Hunchback of Notre-Dame.* Great movie. *(Imitates Charles Laughton)* "Why was I not made of stone, like thee?" *(Realizes it looks like he's imitating Reed's deformity)* I'll return it to him.

REED: Thank you. *(He heads for the door)*

DONALDO: Wait a minute, aa, Mr. Van Druyten. I almost forgot.

REED: Yes?

DONALDO: You've been invited to a church service on Sunday.

REED: Me?

DONALDO: The pastor of that little storefront church asked after you, asked if you could attend.

TOM: So it is going to open.

DONALDO: At least once, this Sunday, ten o'clock.

REED: Asked after me?

DONALDO: Yeah.

REED: Why?

DONALDO: I don't know. The spirit moved him.

REED: I don't think so.

DONALDO: I know it might seem strange.

TOM: Not that strange. A banker used to be a part of the community, go to services with his customers. Makes sense really.

REED: No one's ever . . . I wouldn't know how to do it.

TOM: What do you mean? You wouldn't know how to go to church?

REED: No.

TOM: It's not that hard. You just go. You're making me laugh now. Tell you what. I'll go too.

DONALDO: Look, that's a bit much. You don't have to do that.

TOM: It'll be good for me. If I'm going to do business in this borough, I should go out and meet some of the people. If you need this project to feel a little more indigenous to sell it, then I should probably help by showing up some places. Won't do me any harm.

DONALDO: This reverend is a bit eccentric.

TOM: Good. I could use a bolt from the blue. You let me come along, Reed?

REED: I really don't understand what's happening.

TOM: We're going to church.

REED: Mmm. Would I have to pray?

TOM: Just be respectful. Go along with it. Are you telling me you've never been to any kind of services?

REED: Not really, no.

DONALDO: In your life?

REED: No.

DONALDO: Damn. Not a marriage, not a funeral?

REED: No.

DONALDO: Sorry, I'm being rude.

REED: My parents didn't like religion so we were kept away. I guess it became a habit. Staying away.

TOM: Well, I don't want to press you into something.

DONALDO: Look, I'll respect whatever you want to do, Reed.

TOM: But staying away from every house of worship all your life is pretty extreme. I mean it's a social setting.

DONALDO: I was raised in a church. So for me it's kind of wild you've never been.

TOM: It'd be an experience anyway.

REED: All right. Sure.

DONALDO: Hallelujah! Just kidding.

TOM: We'll get some breakfast afterwards.

REED: I'm glad my father's dead.

DONALDO: What?

REED: I'm glad my father's dead. He wouldn't approve. Nice to meet you. I'll get on this, Mr. Raidenberg.

(Reed exits. The men are uneasy.)

TOM: That was unsettling.

DONALDO: Probably just came out wrong.

TOM: Yeah. Let me ask you. Where you headed?

DONALDO: Back to my office.

TOM: No, no. Big picture.

DONALDO: I don't know.

TOM: Private sector? Mayor's office?

DONALDO: Not finished with the Bronx yet.

TOM: But you will finish. This is the mayor's project.

DONALDO: I know. He's way high on it.

TOM: You know why?

DONALDO: Jobs?

TOM: The mayor loves business. He's a businessman. He loves the deal, he loves the deal maker. That's his earth and the air he breathes. Sometimes we miss the obvious about people. Like goes to like. You a fan of business?

DONALDO: Sure. Absolutely.

TOM: Business is about motion. The key is to constantly reconceive what people need. That keeps society dynamic. When you reshuffle a community, everybody benefits.

DONALDO: Not everybody likes to be reshuffled. What about stability?

TOM: You're right. Good point.

DONALDO: Is it so wrong to stand still a minute, take a pause?

TOM: But we need growth.

DONALDO: Always?

TOM: Ideally.

DONALDO: Cancer is a growth.

TOM: What?

DONALDO: Not that I'm saying that.

TOM: Look. I'm a pie-eyed optimist. Always have been. My guess, you're going to help the Bronx and then you're going to step on to a bigger stage.

DONALDO: Hey, I just go from haircut to haircut.

TOM: A man needs a prize, a pot of gold. You could be a senator. But you need a record of achievement.

DONALDO: Come on. It's a mall. It's a big project, lot of money, but it's not like we're talking about the Louisiana Purchase.

TOM: What's Louisiana got to do with it? Listen. This isn't about a mall. It isn't even about three hundred million dollars. It's about you.

DONALDO: Me.

TOM: You deliver this, we know who you are.

DONALDO: Right. *(Gets up)* I'd better be going.

(Tom stands.)

TOM: Your mother must be something.

DONALDO: My mother?

TOM: Her signature is very strong. I was struck by it. I always think men are made or broken by their mothers. Nice to see you. When you go out, don't tell my secretary.

DONALDO: What?

TOM: What do you think? That I ate the house. *(He laughs)*

Scene 2

A city park. Night. A bench. A lit-up Christmas tree. Under the bench is a half-deflated basketball. Donaldo appears in his winter coat. Music. Something like "Another World" by Antony and the Johnsons. Donaldo touches the tree, smells the needles. Sees the basketball, reminiscences. Does an old move from his days on the court. Pulls his back. Sits on the bench with the ball. Then drops it and lets it limp away. The lights fade.

Scene 3

The storefront church, dark as it was before. Jessie is playing "I Shall Not Be Moved" on the piano. Chester enters in a winter coat.

CHESTER: Here's the day. Start me off singing.

JESSIE:
> I shall not be

CHESTER:
> I shall not be moved

JESSIE:
> I shall not be

CHESTER:
> I shall not be moved.

> *(For Chester, it's nostalgia.)*

CHESTER AND JESSIE:

> Just like a tree that's planted by the water
> I shall not be moved.

(For Jessie, the song is a subdued act of faith. Chester disappears through the curtain, continues to sing from off.)

JESSIE:

> On my way to glory land

CHESTER *(Off)*:

> I shall not be moved

JESSIE:

> On my way to glory land

CHESTER *(Off)*:

> I shall not be moved.

(Chester reappears without his coat and holding a water pitcher and glass.)

CHESTER AND JESSIE:

> Oh like a tree that's planted by the water
> I shall not be moved.

CHESTER: Amen. Hello, Sister Jessie.

JESSIE: Hi, Reverend.

CHESTER: Want some water?

JESSIE: No, thank you.

CHESTER: Bit early.

JESSIE: I needed to settle myself. So you decided to go ahead.

CHESTER: I did.

JESSIE: Glad for you. I know you've been suffering.

CHESTER: I don't know that'll change. But it's good to be in a new day. I invited the bank.

JESSIE: You what?

CHESTER: Seemed right.

JESSIE: You're gonna have your hands full saving those souls.

CHESTER: The service is for everybody. Your husband going to come?

JESSIE: Maybe. Ethan has been sick. Say a prayer for him.

CHESTER: The good Lord hasn't let me pray.

JESSIE: How you gonna hold a service?

CHESTER: I don't know.

JESSIE: I know that you contain spiritual power, Reverend Kimmich. Use it today.

CHESTER: I don't feel ready. Here it is, Sunday. I thought it would come to me but it hasn't.

JESSIE: It will.

(Ethan comes in.)

ETHAN: Hey there.

CHESTER: Hi, Mr. Goldklang.

JESSIE: There's my man.

(Ethan is beaming, full of news.)

ETHAN: Guess what? My doctor died!

JESSIE: Stedman?

ETHAN: Dead. Didn't wake up this morning.

JESSIE: You upset?

ETHAN: Do I look upset? He said I'd die, boom, he died. You know what I call that? *(Gives a gleeful finger in Stedman's direction)* Justice.

JESSIE: You should sit down. You don't look that good.

ETHAN: I look better than Stedman.

JESSIE: Maybe we should go to the hospital.

ETHAN: I've been to the hospital and I'm taking the meds. This is a good day. I know what's coming.

CHESTER: How you doing?

ETHAN: Perfect. I'm here. So you're making a move. Good for you. Am I blind or can we turn on some lights?

CHESTER: Of course.

ETHAN: To quote a bestseller: Let there be light.

(Jessie and Chester turn on some lights.)

That's better.

JESSIE: I should have come down and cleaned.

ETHAN: What's a little dust? I'll wipe the seats. *(He wipes with a handkerchief)* I've never attended a Pentecostal service. How does it go?

CHESTER: I know how I used to do it, but I don't know how I do it now.

ETHAN: I feel that way about masturbation.

JESSIE: Ethan!

ETHAN: I know. I'm in church.

JESSIE: Don't go mental on me.

ETHAN: It might be fun.

CHESTER: Are you a religious man?

ETHAN: I hate religion.

JESSIE: You shut up now.

ETHAN: She believes for both of us. I'm a secular Jew. Nobody knows what that is, but there's a lot of us.

(The door opens tentatively. Tom enters.)

TOM: Is this the Divine Plan For Salvation Church?

ETHAN: Is it?

CHESTER: It is.

ETHAN: It is? It has a name? I didn't know it had a name.

TOM: It has a phone number, too. But nobody answers.

CHESTER: I unplugged it long since.

TOM: Hi. I'm Tom Raidenberg.

ETHAN: Ethan Goldklang.

TOM: Ethan Goldklang. Great name.

ETHAN: You've got to be kidding.

TOM: Great to meet you.

ETHAN: And this is my wife, Jessie Cortez.

JESSIE: Nice to meet you.

TOM: A pleasure.

ETHAN: You look like you're in the wrong neighborhood.

TOM: No, I love this part of town. And you're the Reverend Kimmich?

CHESTER: Yes, sir.

TOM: Nice to make your acquaintance.

CHESTER: Nice to meet you. Where'd you learn to wear clothes like that? You're a handsome man.

TOM: God bless you, Reverend. Thank you.

CHESTER: You're like an actor playing the part of an ordinary person.

TOM: I don't know what to say to that. Thank you I guess.

CHESTER: I'd better put my jacket on. I don't look good enough to be in the same room with you.

(Chester exits as Tom says:)

TOM: You look fine. I wish I looked so good. *(To Ethan)* Nice guy.

ETHAN: Yeah, he's nuts.

(Reed enters. He has a small bunch of cheap flowers and an envelope.)

Look at this one. Hey, you I know. What are you doing here?

REED: Uh . . .

ETHAN: You're the guy from the bank.

TOM: Hello, Reed.

ETHAN: You know each other?

TOM: We're colleagues.

ETHAN: TWO bankers. An accumulation of bankers.

JESSIE: The reverend invited them.

REED: Good morning, Mr. Raidenberg.

TOM: Good morning.

ETHAN: Loan officer, remember me? The cubicle? I was the one on the floor.

REED: I remember you.

ETHAN: Are you surprised to see me alive?

REED: Aaa. I don't know.

ETHAN: I'm not sorry I yelled at you.

JESSIE: You did what?

ETHAN: He was being a hard-ass. How was the cake?

REED: I threw it away.

ETHAN: The whole cake? You didn't taste it?! You're a crazy bastid.

JESSIE: You threw my cake away?

REED: I can't accept gifts.

TOM: Reed. You can accept a cake.

JESSIE: I forgive you. *(Picks up a shopping bag)* And you're in luck. I have another one right here.

REED: Oh no.

JESSIE: There's five eggs in that cake.

ETHAN: And two sticks of butter.

REED: I can't.

TOM: Reed. Take the cake.

(Reed takes it.)

REED: Thank you.

JESSIE: Welcome. There's paper plates and all in there. Nice way to make friends.

ETHAN: You could offer me a piece.

JESSIE: Do not give this man cake!

REED: Duly noted.

(Chester enters in a jacket.)

CHESTER: Welcome. I'm Chester Kimmich. The pastor here.

REED: Reed Van Druyten.

ETHAN: Van Druyten. That German?

REED: Dutch.

ETHAN: Just checking. The Dutch. You bought Manhattan. What, now you're back for the Bronx?

JESSIE: Ethan, where's your manners?

ETHAN: Why are bankers here?

REED: I was invited.

JESSIE: They were invited.

CHESTER: That's right. I invited them. *(He indicates flowers)* Those for the church?

REED: I didn't know what was appropriate. Yes.

CHESTER: Thank you. I'll put them in some water. Flowers in the winter. Always lifts the heart. *(He takes the flowers, exits)*

ETHAN: Flowers in the winter, and money changers in the temple. I can't believe you have the chutzpah to show up here.

(Donaldo enters.)

Hey, Donaldo.

DONALDO: Hey, Ethan, you look better. Your color's better.

ETHAN: Shut up, I'm half dead. Hey, look at this. Bankers in church.

DONALDO: Well, we all have to be some place, why not church? Good morning, Reed! Looking good! Glad you got here. It's all coming together, that Christmas energy. *(Sings) Feliz Navidad, Feliz Navidad.* All my favorite people. Good morning, Tom!

TOM: Good morning, Donaldo.

DONALDO: Happy Sunday, Jessie!

JESSIE: Happy Sunday!

DONALDO: Sorry I was late. The kids were crazy.

TOM: No problem. I found it.

DONALDO: I feel terrible I wasn't here to do introductions. *(To Ethan and Jessie)* Tom's the CEO of First Circle Bank.

JESSIE: Oh-h-h.

ETHAN *(Overlapping)*: Oh-h-h. The CEO, no less.

TOM: I heard there was a service. I wanted to be a part of it.

ETHAN: Really? Why?

TOM: I don't know. It's the holidays. Goodwill.

ETHAN: You're looking for goodwill here?

JESSIE: Maybe he's looking to be saved.

ETHAN: Good luck with that.

DONALDO: And you met Jessie Cortez?

JESSIE: We just met.

TOM: I can understand your animosity, Mr. Goldklang, given what you know. But I assure you I'm not insensitive. I wouldn't be here if I didn't have ameliorating news.

ETHAN: What kind of news?

DONALDO: News of what nature?

TOM: I should say WE have some news to share with you, Miss Cortez.

JESSIE *(To Ethan)*: Oh God, this is it.

DONALDO: We? Should I know what you're about to say?

TOM: No. This works. I was going to bring you up to speed before we came in, but now will do.

JESSIE: Would you tell us?

TOM: Donaldo, your intercession on Ms. Cortez' behalf was successful.

DONALDO: Are we in the same conversation?

TOM: We are. It's not going to be necessary to foreclose on your house.

JESSIE: What?

ETHAN: We're getting the extension?

TOM: No. No extension.

JESSIE: No extension? Then what are you talking about?

TOM: We're not going to foreclose at all.

ETHAN: Why not?

DONALDO: Tom, what's going on?

JESSIE: Don't mess with me!

TOM: I'm not messing with you. Reed, am I accurate?

REED: Yes.

JESSIE: Is this one of those reality shows? 'Cause I'll kill you both!

REED: Uh . . .

DONALDO *(To Tom)*: Talk to me.

JESSIE: Is this real?

TOM: It's real.

JESSIE: But we haven't even had the service yet. Reverend! Donaldo, you did it!

DONALDO: Did what?

JESSIE: You stopped the bank.

DONALDO: No, I didn't. *(To Tom)* She owes you money. What are you, Santa Claus?

TOM: Not really.

JESSIE: Are you hearing this, Ethan?

ETHAN: Don't get excited. There has to be something wrong with it.

TOM: Reed, give 'em the news.

REED: There's going to be a refund.

JESSIE: To who?

ETHAN: What do you mean, a refund?

REED: I have some paperwork for you. You should have it looked over. The note's going to be reissued and written off.

JESSIE: I feel lightheaded.

(Ethan and Tom catch Jessie as she collapses into a chair.)

ETHAN AND TOM: Whoa!

ETHAN: What do you mean, a refund?

REED: You get back the balloon payment. The debt's forgiven.

(Chester reenters with the flowers in a little vase.)

CHESTER: You called, Sister?

JESSIE: Reverend, this man says he's forgiving me.

CHESTER: Did you do him wrong?

JESSIE: No, it's not like that.

CHESTER: Then what's he forgiving you for?

JESSIE: It's some kind of a good thing.

ETHAN: What happens to the second mortgage?

REED: There won't be a second mortgage. It will be forgiven.

CHESTER: There he goes. He's forgiving you again. What for?

REED: It's a term.

CHESTER: There must be something to it.

DONALDO: He's forgiving her for taking his money and not giving it back.

JESSIE: You don't have to put it like that.

ETHAN: It's the truth.

CHESTER: Is that right?

REED: It's not my money.

CHESTER: Well then, whose money is it?

REED: The bank's.

ETHAN: Oh, we're back to that again?

JESSIE: Leave off him! This is the answer to my prayers! Reed, you are coming to my house for dinner tonight!

(She embraces him. He freaks, scurrying away.)

REED: PLEASE! Don't touch me! *(Calming)* I have dinner plans.

JESSIE: Okay. Another time then. *(To Ethan, referring to Reed)* He's a little whacky.

ETHAN: Give him room. He's been drinking.

JESSIE: I feel like I've been drinking. I have to sit down again.

REED: Those documents explain everything.

(Ethan has been looking them over.)

ETHAN: They look all right to me. *(He hands the documents to Jessie)*

REED: I've never been in a church before. Are we in the service now?

CHESTER: Not yet.

DONALDO: No, this is just people socializing.

JESSIE: Donaldo, you delivered. I don't know how to thank you.

DONALDO: Don't thank me.

JESSIE: Why didn't you tell me?

DONALDO: I didn't know.

TOM: Come on. You had an inkling.

DONALDO: Look, I can't take credit for this. You want to thank somebody, thank the bank.

JESSIE: Okay, who's the bank?

ETHAN: Good luck getting an answer to that.

DONALDO: Tom here's the bank, I guess.

JESSIE: You're the bank?

TOM: Me? I'm just a working stiff. Don't be modest, Donaldo. This is because of your efforts.

DONALDO: All I did, all I set out to do was to talk to your loan officer, and then Tom got interested.

TOM: Obviously, without Mr. Calderon's efforts to make us aware of the particulars of this loan . . . Well, let's just say, he helped us to get it right.

DONALDO: You're being too generous. Not to be snappish, Tom, but you did the talking and that's all that happened. Talking. Nothing was resolved. This is your good deed.

TOM: Somebody's being modest. I didn't do a thing. Reed?

REED: I don't really understand.

TOM: Let's just focus on the good news then.

JESSIE *(Church lady)*: The good news!

TOM: You're not losing your house.

JESSIE: Praise God!

TOM: Once those papers are signed.

JESSIE: Give me a pen, Ethan.

ETHAN: I don't have a pen.

DONALDO: Don't sign that yet.

JESSIE: Why not?

DONALDO: They should be looked over.

TOM: You'll need a notary anyway.

REED: I'm a notary.

ETHAN: I've got to be missing something.

DONALDO: Can I see those? *(He brusquely takes the papers from Jessie and sits a few chairs away)*

ETHAN: I don't get it. There's got to be a catch.

TOM: When well-intentioned people come together, anything is possible. We can get a lot done, this and more. Progress. Motion.

JESSIE: Motion! Hallelujah!

(Donaldo's uneasy. He doesn't look at the papers.)

TOM: I like this little church.

ETHAN: Maybe you should put in a cash machine.

TOM: Funny guy! Maybe I should.

JESSIE: Donaldo, what are you doing with those papers?

DONALDO: I'm looking them over.

JESSIE: No you're not. You're just holding them.

DONALDO: I'll get to it.

TOM: This is good for everybody, Donaldo.

ETHAN: It gets your mother off the hook.

DONALDO: My mother? Yeah. She'll be relieved.

JESSIE: Your mother thinks you're a great man.

DONALDO: My mother's a damn fool.

TOM: I'd like to meet your mother at some point.

DONALDO: She has an impractical streak.

TOM: You all right?

DONALDO: Yeah. Things are just moving a little ahead of me.

TOM: I meant to tell you privately, but you were late.

DONALDO: It's fine. I'm just . . . You know what? I'm off track. I came here for a service.

JESSIE: I'm ready for that!

ETHAN: There's got to be a catch.

JESSIE: Don't look a miracle in the mouth.

DONALDO: Enough. I came here to hear a preacher preach. Enough about worldly stuff. Mortgages and whatnot. I'm gonna shake it off. You do the same.

JESSIE: You're right, Donaldo.

DONALDO: Reverend? I guess we could use a little spiritual leadership. Where do you want us?

CHESTER: Well, all right. Should we take a seat? Go ahead and sit down. Anywhere's good. Everybody comfortable?

JESSIE: I've been waiting for this day.

CHESTER: Me too, and here it is. *(To Reed)* Do I understand that you're a stranger to any form of worship, sir?

REED: Is this the service?

CHESTER: Yes, it is.

REED: I don't want to participate. I'm just here.

CHESTER: This is how it's done. Little give and take. Sometimes I'm looking for a bit of a person's experience. Are you carrying a burden, friend?

REED: Please. Ask somebody else.

CHESTER: Because I am. I've lost my way. Makes me feel sick. The good Lord took away my feeling of direction. Anybody here ever feel like that?

(Jessie softly answers yes.)

Anybody here ever feel the old ways don't work no more, the habit of optimism is just gone?

DONALDO: Optimism isn't always good.

CHESTER: Does that mean you don't have any?

DONALDO: You can't always rely on uplift to get you through.

CHESTER: My positivity came from praying and I can't pray.

DONALDO: Maybe you were talking to yourself.

CHESTER: No. I have faith.

DONALDO: Then what's the problem?

CHESTER: I am here to testify: You can have faith, recognize the hand of God, believe in salvation, and still hate life. What if God plucks you like a chess piece from the board and puts you in that dead border around the game? You see everything, but at the direction of the Almighty Force, you are relegated to be no more than a witness to the work and the truth of others. Does anybody here besides me feel dead?

JESSIE: Dead?

DONALDO: What kind of question is that?

CHESTER: When the hurricane took New Orleans and negated my world, in a way I was lucky, because I could point to the hurricane. That's the storm that stopped my life. How bad is it when you can't point 'cause there's nothing? There's nothing there. The house looks fine but you can't live in it. Does anybody besides me feel dead?

(Reed raises his hand.)

ETHAN: You do?
TOM: Reed?
REED: Yes?
TOM: You don't have to speak.

(Reed addresses Chester with bitterness.)

REED: What is this?
CHESTER: A voice in my soul asked for you to come here today, sir. I'm a pastor, a preacher, but I can't pray. Why do you feel dead?
REED: Because I am dead.
CHESTER: Man says he's dead.
JESSIE: No, he's not. What are you talking about? Goodness gracious, you're not dead.
REED: Yes I am.
TOM *(To Donaldo)*: I think I should get him out of here.
DONALDO: Why don't you wait on that, Tom. He's got a right to take up some space.
TOM: Okay.
DONALDO: Go on, Reed.
REED: There was a girl. She was pretty. It didn't work out. It didn't work out. That's all. She . . . LEFT!
DONALDO: I'm sorry.

(Silence.)

CHESTER: Your pain and your silence are filling up this whole place, friend.

(Silence. Reed is resisting speaking.)

TOM: Look, may I suggest I take him home.

DONALDO: Tom, everybody has a right to some time.

TOM: Of course.

REED: Mmm. I . . .

DONALDO: I'm here.

REED: You are?

DONALDO: Yeah, you got something?

REED: Yes.

DONALDO: Then say it.

REED: You don't want it.

DONALDO: Yes I do.

REED: Okay. I have to work for this prick. I can't feel half my face. My wife . . . is worse than dead. She's in prison. She hates. I hate myself.

JESSIE: No hate. There's love in this room.

DONALDO: Let him speak.

JESSIE: It's not right.

REED: It's right. I'm broken. I have nothing. Look at me. Don't you get it? "Why was I not made of stone?"

ETHAN *(Gently)*: Quasimodo.

REED: "Why was I not made of stone?" *(Indicating Tom)* Like thee?

TOM: Me? That's enough! I'm sorry for his, this crazy outburst.

ETHAN: He's fine.

JESSIE: He's a little crazy.

TOM: Reed . . .

CHESTER: A man has to be able to talk.

DONALDO *(To Tom)*: I know it's at your expense, Tom, but let it go.

JESSIE *(To Reed)*: You're gonna be all right.

DONALDO *(To Tom)*: Give him a pass. Look at him. People have problems.

ETHAN *(To Tom)*: You're in the Bronx now.

TOM: You're drunk, aren't you?

REED *(To Tom)*: Look at me. I was you.

TOM: I don't drink. What are you talking about?

REED *(To Chester, referring to himself and Tom)*: We're the witch doctors. What are we selling? What the hell is it? Smoke! And then we go. We're gone. Don't look to see us next week. No.

TOM: I didn't realize he drinks.

DONALDO: He's all right.

REED: You call this drunk, Mr. Raidenberg? Do you ever look behind you? Take a tip from me. Don't. There's nothing there.

JESSIE: You need to take my hand.

REED: What?

JESSIE: Take it.

(Reed takes her hand, starts to silently break down. He sits beside her.)

You stay by me now.

REED: Yes, ma'am.

TOM *(To Jessie)*: Thank you.

JESSIE: I don't mind. Reverend Kimmich, this man's in pain.

CHESTER: I'm affected now. Is anybody else affected?

ETHAN: Sure.

(Jessie murmurs yes.)

DONALDO: Yeah.

TOM: I'm sorry I brought him . . .

DONALDO: I'm not. He's all right.

CHESTER *(To Tom)*: What about you, sir? Are you affected?

TOM: Of course.

CHESTER: How?

TOM: The man works for me.

CHESTER: Does he do a good job?

TOM: I'm embarrassed by his behavior.

REED: I do my job. I'm doing it right now. I brought your paper-work.

CHESTER: Are you feeling him?

TOM: Certainly. But I expect things of people as well. Civility, for instance.

REED: You expect all kinds of things.

JESSIE: Why you on him? He's saving my house.

REED: He never saved anybody. *(J'accuse!)* Look at you. You don't even know.

TOM: Oh, he's at it again.

REED: You can't even imagine it, can you? You can't imagine it happening to you.

TOM: What are you talking about?

REED: Do you think because you get up early and get home late, do you think that means you're good?

TOM: You don't know anything about my life.

REED: Oh I do, yes.

TOM: No, you don't.

REED: Like looking in the mirror, I know you.

TOM: You're nuts.

REED: Look at you, you empty stiff! And the rest of you. Sitting there like . . . Mohicans.

TOM: *The Last of the Mohicans*?

ETHAN: That's a great book.

REED: May I speak?

CHESTER: Go ahead, brother. Testify.

REED: Reverend, good question you had. Why WAS this woman forgiven? *(To Jessie)* Wonder where your debt's gone, miss? Debts don't just disappear.

JESSIE: I prayed and my prayers were answered.

REED: It's a miracle. Do you believe in miracles, Mr. Calderon?

DONALDO: I used to.

REED: Should I stop?

DONALDO: Not on my account.

REED: Something's not right.

TOM: What's not right is this man, who is ungrateful for his job. And what is right is this house is saved from foreclosure. You were in trouble. We took note.

REED: We sold her a note. No way she could pay it back. We knew that.

TOM: What are you talking about? We had collateral.

REED: Right, collateral! Paper. The box was checked. The house. Take the house. *(To all but Tom)* You don't step on us and step on us HARD, we'll take all your houses! Wake up. We're a gang. Thugs! *(To Ethan)* 'Member what you said, Mr. Goldklang? Bad advice is a breach, a debt.

TOM: Leave these good people alone!

REED: Bad advice is a debt!

ETHAN: I said that. He's quoting me.

REED: I listen. Maybe I don't look like I'm listening because I'm deformed.

JESSIE: You look all right. But what are you talking about?

REED: Your mortgage.

(Donaldo takes the papers out of the envelope and starts reading.)

JESSIE: What about it?

REED: You get money, somebody pays somehow. Right, Mr. Borough President?

DONALDO: What's your point?

REED: Are you feeling obligated?

TOM: Reed.

REED *(To Donaldo)*: Should I go on?

TOM: No! You're a drunk and you think life is a cheat.

REED: No, I think you're a cheat! Throwing your net over people.

TOM: You thought you'd hit the jackpot and you got stupid. Now you're bitter.

REED: She owes you thirty thousand dollars plus interest. And then she doesn't. You wouldn't forgive your mother that kind of money unless there was a fat fee somewhere. The fee on three hundred million for the mall.

ETHAN *(Eureka)*: There's the catch! *(He goes to Jessie)*

TOM: There is no catch. The mall is a great project.

REED: You're a pig.

ETHAN: Jessie . . .

TOM: You're an alcoholic. He's an alcoholic!

JESSIE: My mother was an alcoholic!

TOM: Shit. Donaldo, I'm sorry.

DONALDO: For what?

TOM *(Referring to Reed)*: Him.

(Ethan is earnestly conferring with Jessie.)

ETHAN: Jessie.

REED *(To Tom)*: Don't apologize for me!

ETHAN: It's a bribe.

TOM *(To Reed)*: Somebody has to.

REED: Trying to reel him in with your enticements. "Our refi efforts . . ." Please! You have him by the balls. Page eighteen. Your mother's signature as guarantor!

TOM: Are you leaving?

REED: I don't think so. No. I like church.

TOM: Then I am.

REED: You're already gone. You were never here.

DONALDO: All right, Reed, that's enough.

REED: Okay.

TOM: Donaldo, we can take this up later. I'm very sorry.

DONALDO: For what?

TOM: The theatrics.

DONALDO: No, me too. *(Referring to the papers)* This is . . . generous stuff.

JESSIE: It is?

DONALDO: Yeah.

TOM: I thought I lost you there for a minute.

DONALDO: No.

TOM: I know I can be a bit clumsy, but I was affected by all this. I am affected. We're all on the same side.

REED: No, we're not.

TOM: Well, those of us who are sane.

DONALDO: I'm sorry if I was . . . If I appeared unappreciative. I just lost my bearings a bit.

TOM: No worries. It was going by pretty fast. I should have told you privately. I'll call you. We're good, right?

DONALDO: Right.

TOM: Right?

DONALDO: Yes.

TOM: Good. It'll all work out. God bless. *(He puts a bill on the piano)* For the collection.

REED: Paper.

(Tom goes to the door, stops, addresses Reed.)

TOM: Obviously, you don't need to come in tomorrow.

CHESTER: You don't have to go.

TOM: Peace. *(He goes)*

CHESTER: People are telling the truth. Man just lost his job. I'm affected. Anybody else affected?

JESSIE: Yes. *(Looks at the bill)* He left a hundred-dollar bill.

DONALDO: Did he? Of course he did.

REED: He'll write it off.

ETHAN *(To Donaldo)*: Why did you do that?

DONALDO: What?

ETHAN: Sell yourself down the river.

DONALDO: I just told him what he wanted to hear.

ETHAN: But what are you actually going to do?

DONALDO: Who cares? It's just another day. *(Referring to Reed)* He's the man.

ETHAN: Him? He's unemployed. *(To Reed)* Hey pal, it'll be all right.

REED: What will?

ETHAN: A job isn't much.

DONALDO: It's just a suit of clothes.

JESSIE: I got to say, no job's worth your balls.

ETHAN *(To Reed)*: That's right. At least you got your balls.

REED: No. No balls.

CHESTER: That isn't for you to say.

JESSIE: God gave you balls and I'd say you still got 'em, mister.

REED: I have no idea what's going on.

ETHAN: Maybe you're a great man. Maybe that's what's going on.

REED: Uh . . .

DONALDO: Where's our sermon, Reverend?

CHESTER: I think the fire's in you. You give it.

DONALDO: Me? I haven't got a decent thing to say.

REED: That's 'cause your mother's still the guarantor on that loan. *(To Jessie)* Until you sign those papers.

JESSIE: Donaldo, lay it out for me. What's going on?

DONALDO: If you're so hot to know, why don't you run after that fat cat and ask him.

JESSIE: What are you mad at me for?

DONALDO: Because you believe in miracles and other people pay. You want me to give a sermon? I can do that. I'm bored. I'm so goddamn bored with this modern world. There's a hole in the ground in front of me. When I was a kid, I was poor. The city had a thing for poor kids, sent them to the country. I'd never been out of the Bronx, and they bussed me up to a camp on a lake. One night when I was sleeping, a counselor woke me up. When I went outside, though it was the middle of the night, the whole camp was up, and they took us down to the lake. A boy'd gone missing. And the whole camp, and other camps that were on the lake, they were all searching for him in the dark. There were all kinds of flashlights going in the woods and out on the water, rowboats and canoes and they had flashlights, too. All looking for one lost boy. I looked from that, all those lights in the lower night, and found my eyes lifting to the sky. And what I saw there I will never forget. The sky was overburdened with stars, like a miracle. It was impossible. I'd never seen the like in my young life. Thousands, millions of stars, pouring out of everywhere, like the cavalry, like a saving army. And it seemed to me that HEAVEN was joining earth, and that everything in time and space and spirit and flesh had joined together in service to finding this lost child. Of course I thought of my father, and I knew that this was his work and his reason, and I thought of the Good Shepherd going after the one and leaving the ninety-nine. And in that moment in the night, I knew how it all worked, the mechanics of this world and the next. And I was so moved, and felt safe in a way I wish I could share with every man and woman I ever met. But then I came back to the city, and what was clear became obscure, and what life required of me was smaller than what I had seen, and over time, my vision left me utterly and I entered a smaller world. The world of cash and carry. And I have lived there ever since. To my sadness. And that's why anything I do is wrong. And I am oppressed by a lifelong emptiness. *(He's finished with the sermon; gives Jessie the envelope)* Here, Jessie. I read it. It's fine. You'll need a notary to sign.

REED: I'm a notary.

JESSIE: What happens to you?

DONALDO: Good things. I look good.

ETHAN: I don't think you should sign it.

JESSIE: But where will we live?

ETHAN: All I need is great book, a good umbrella, and you beside me, singing in the wilderness.

(Jessie caresses Ethan.)

JESSIE: Always, baby. Always.

CHESTER *(To Donaldo)*: You're a leader.

DONALDO: No, I'm not. I'm a politician.

CHESTER: You're a preacher.

DONALDO: No. You're the preacher and even you can't preach. Everything's money now.

CHESTER: No, there's a need for some things to be said.

DONALDO: Like what?

CHESTER: You can't let a pack of jackals crazy for money lead the way.

DONALDO: Come on, it's all money.

CHESTER: Money is just a fool's dream, my brother, and you know it.

DONALDO: I don't know anything.

CHESTER: A fool's dream of a better world. Don't let 'em deceive you with that. Yes, we long to be away from the pain of existence.

JESSIE: Escape this world.

CHESTER: We look up at the wonders of the sky, and ache with the desire to fly there.

REED: Yes.

CHESTER: What we forget is we ourselves are in the heavens. We forget that the earth is itself in the sky.

ETHAN: That's true.

CHESTER: Perhaps someone looks up at us, and aches to be where we are.

DONALDO: I look up.

CHESTER: I know you do, pilgrim, but we are already home. We are already where we long to be. But we forget. Twisted men have told us money is a refuge from pain . . .

REED: A sanctuary?

CHESTER: That's right, brother! But no house can protect you from death. Do you hear that?

JESSIE: I hear you but I'm weak.

CHESTER: And I'm here to tell you no house can make you strong. Not greed, not mindless activity. Neither is this church a shelter. Only our humanity, our common soul, can provide safe haven.

REED: The soul.

CHESTER: That's right. This soul we share. We got to take care of each other. Do you hear what I'm saying?

JESSIE: Yes I do.

ETHAN: You know, I have to say, either I just became a member of the Divine Plan For Salvation Church, or you just became a secular Jew.

JESSIE: Either way, I say amen.

CHESTER: Amen back to you! Donaldo, you saw the truth as a child and preached it right here as a man. It is a unanalyzable fact that when the many commit to caring for the few that all of us achieve nobility, and our lives meaning. You knew that once.

(Donaldo stands apart.)

DONALDO: But how do I know it again? How do I know it now?

CHESTER: Stand still. Let the spirit find you.

(Jessie moves to the piano and begins to play. She sings, and the others join in.)

JESSIE:

> I shall not be
> I shall not be moved
> I shall not be

JESSIE AND CHESTER:

> Shall not be moved
> Oh like a tree that's planted by the water
> I shall not be moved.

REED: I'd like to learn that tune. Could you sing it again?

DONALDO: Wait. Let me.

> I shall not be
> I shall not be moved

I shall not be
I shall not be . . .

(His voice breaks.)

I don't want to do this alone. Help me.

(They start the song again. Even Ethan joins in. As the song moves toward conclusion, Chester walks toward Donaldo. Donaldo meets him. They embrace.)

END OF PLAY

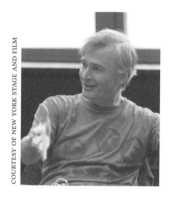

JOHN PATRICK SHANLEY is the author of numerous plays, including *Doubt: A Parable* (winner of the Pulitzer Prize and Tony Award for Best Play), *Outside Mullingar* (Tony Award nomination for Best Play), *Danny and the Deep Blue Sea, Beggars in the House of Plenty, Dirty Story, Where's My Money?, Four Dogs and a Bone, Defiance* and *Storefront Church*. His sole television outing resulted in an Emmy nomination for *Live from Baghdad* (HBO). In the arena of film, *Moonstruck* garnered him an Academy Award for Best Original Screenplay. Mr. Shanley wrote and directed both *Joe Versus the Volcano* and *Doubt*; the latter earned five Oscar nominations, including Best Adapted Screenplay. In 2008, the Writers Guild of America recognized Mr. Shanley's contribution to film with a Lifetime Achievement Award.